COLORING BOOK

Quyumta elitelta!
(Let's all learn together!)

Atqa (My name is)

WELCOME TO THE YUP'IK ALPHABET COLORING BOOK

Welcome to the Yup'ik Alphabet Coloring Book, a delightful journey through the unique sounds and symbols of the Yup'ik language! Created with love and dedication by Nikki Corbett and Katie O'Connor, founders of Ciuneq, LLC, this book is a celebration of Yup'ik culture and heritage.

About the Yup'ik Alphabet: The Yup'ik language is rich with tradition and history, and its alphabet reflects the deep connection between the Yup'ik people and the natural world around them. Each letter of the Yup'ik alphabet is represented by a unique symbol, many of which are inspired by animals, plants, and elements of the Arctic landscape.

About this Coloring Book: In these pages, you will find 27 beautifully illustrated images, each corresponding to a letter of the Yup'ik alphabet. From "A" for "Akutaq" to "Y" for "Yaaruin" (storyknife), every page offers an opportunity to explore Yup'ik words and culture while expressing your creativity through coloring.

Note to Readers: We hope you enjoy this Yup'ik Alphabet Coloring Book as much as we enjoyed creating it. May it inspire curiosity, creativity, and a deeper appreciation for the beauty of the Yup'ik language and culture.

QUYANA CAKNEQ FOR JOINING US ON THIS COLORFUL ADVENTURE!

aa

Aańa

E

Egturyaq

g

Agluryaq

gg

Kegginaquq

!kamraq

K

Kaviaq

L

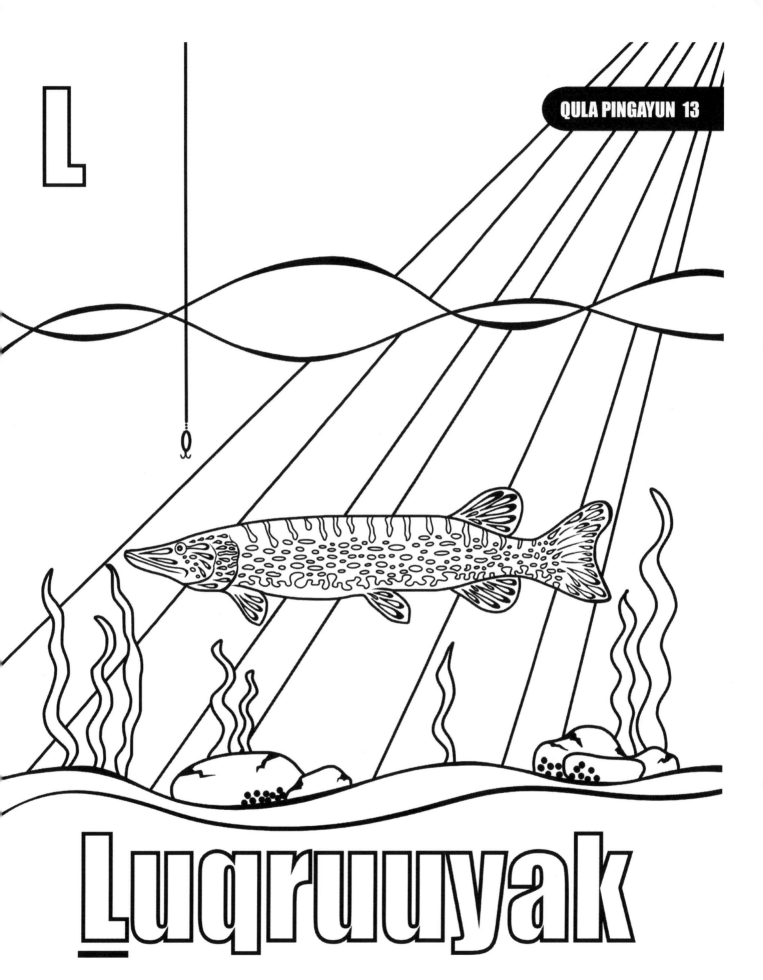

Luqruuyak

Ellalluk

M

Maqivik

N

Nasqurrun

ng

Tengssuun

P

Paluqtaq

Q

Qaspeq

r

Iraluq

rr

Egamaa<u>rr</u>luk

S

Asveq

T

Tulukaruk

U

Uluaq

uu

Ipuun

VV

Kuù̱Wiaq

W

Wiinga

Y

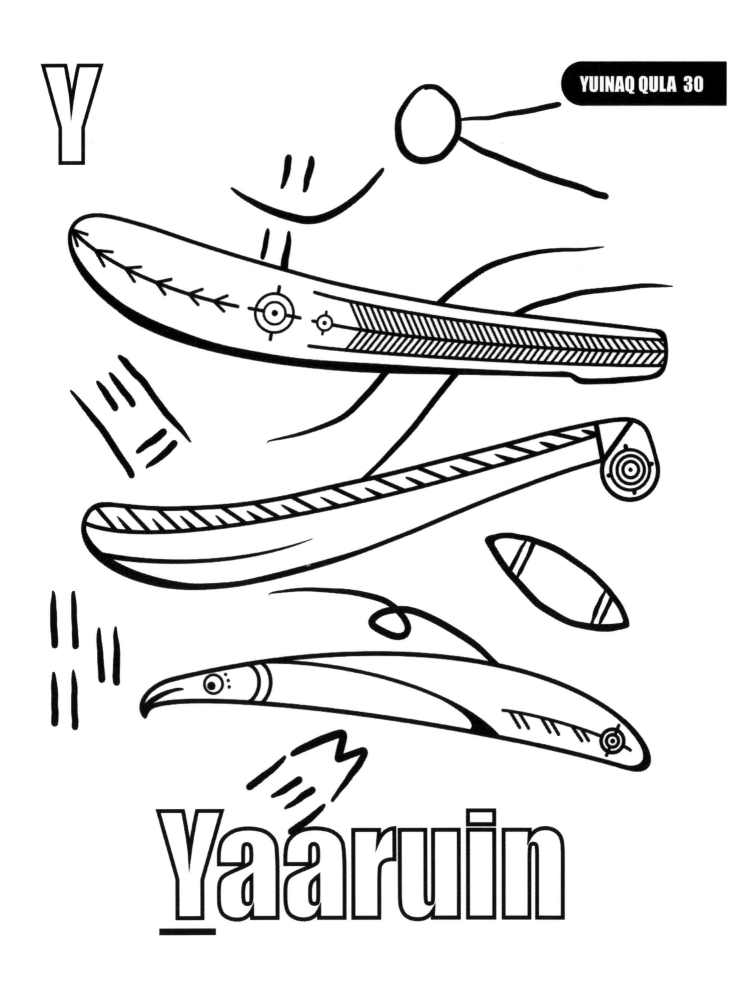

Y̲aaruin

GLOSSARY

Akutaq- Mixture "Eskimo ice cream," a mixture of berries, sugar, seal oil, shortening, fish, meat, etc.

Aana- Mom

Cauyaq- Drum

Egturyaq (also kegturyaq)- Mosquito

Agluryaq- Rainbow

Kegginaquq- Mask

Ikamraq- Sled, dog sled; by extension snowmachine, automobile, taxi; also dual for one sled

Iik- Eyes

Kaviaq- Red fox

Luqruuyak- Northern pike

Ellalluk- Rain

Maqivik- Steambath house

Nasqurrun- Dance headdress; crown

Tengssuun- Airplane

Paluqtaq- Beaver

Qaspeq- Thin hooded garment, usually of cloth, worn as a parka cover, jacket or dress

Iraluq- Moon or month

Egamaarrluk- Partially dried fish, boiled for eating

Asveq- Walrus

Assaliaq- Frybread other fried food; pancake

Tulukaruk- Raven

Uluaq- Traditional Eskimo-style woman's knife shaped like a broad wedge set in a handle opposite the arc-shaped edge, semilunar knife; sometimes called 'ulu' in English

Ipuun- Ladle

Evegtaq- Bumblebee

Kuuvviaq- Coffee

Wiinga- I, me (personal pronoun)

Yaaruin- Story knife

The definitions are taken from the Yup'ik Eskimo Dictionary compiled by Steven A. Jacobsen

YUP'IK ALPHABET CHART

The Yup'ik language is a complex and unique one in that it is very difficult to create a chart for non-Yup'ik speakers to understand. In the Yup'ik language the endings indicate if it is referring to one (q), two (k), three or more (t).

ASVEQ

One (1)

ASVEREK

Two (2)

ASVERET

Three (3)
Or more

YUP'IK PHRASES

Waqaa- Hello
Cangacit?- How are you?
Assirtua- I am good
Quyana- Thank you
Piuraa- Bye
Kenkamken- I love you

QUYANA CAKNEQ

ACKNOWLEDGMENTS

Quyana to all those who contributed to the creation of this Yup'ik Alphabet coloring book.

Quyana to my panik Amaarculi for lighting the fire within me.

Quyana to my aipaq for steadfastly standing by my side throughout this journey.

Quyana to Jenine Heakin, Christopher (Egalaaq) Liu, Arnaq Marie Meade, and Ayaprun Loddie Jones for their invaluable guidance and support.

Quyana to Katie O'Connor for believing in our vision and for bringing her remarkable artistic talents to this project.

Special thanks to David Angaiak for the contribution of "Kegginaquq" and for allowing us to use your image and mask carving in our coloring book.

This book would not have been possible without the dedication, encouragement, and expertise of each of you.

ABOUT

About the Author: Nikki "Quluqaaq" Corbett

Nikki Corbett is a passionate advocate for Indigenous languages and cultures, with a particular focus on preserving and promoting the Yup'ik language. Born and raised in a Yup'ik community, Nikki has always felt a deep connection to her heritage and strives to share its beauty with the world. With a background in education and a love for storytelling, Nikki brings a wealth of knowledge and creativity to her work. Through her collaboration with Ciuneq, LLC, Nikki aims to inspire children and learners of all ages to explore the wonders of the Yup'ik language and culture.

About the Illustrator: Katie O'Connor

Katie O'Connor is a talented artist with a flair for capturing the essence of cultural diversity and tradition. With a background in fine arts and illustration, Katie's work is characterized by its vibrant colors, intricate details, and heartfelt storytelling. Inspired by her own experiences and travels, Katie brings a unique perspective to her illustrations, infusing each piece with warmth, humor, and authenticity. As the illustrator for the Yup'ik Alphabet coloring book, Katie's captivating artwork breathes life into the pages, inviting readers to embark on a colorful journey through the world of the Yup'ik language.

Made in the USA
Columbia, SC
31 October 2024

45414035R00039